" I opened Teresa's book Just Breathe as soon as I got home from our coffee and did not get up from my chair until I had read every word. I couldn't put it down. A more beautiful story of restoration and redemption after the hideous thievery of her childhood by a sexually abusive grandfather, I have never read. Talk about following God one yes at a time into wholeness! "

---

CONNIE CAVANAUGH – AUTHOR/SPEAKER
*"FOLLOWING GOD ONE YES AT A TIME".*

# Just Breathe

## Hope Beyond Hurt

TERESA M RILLING

Produced by:

FriesenPress
Suite 300 – 852 Fort Street
Victoria, BC, Canada V8W 1H8

www.friesenpress.com

Distributed to the trade by The Ingram Book Company

Dedication: I dedicate this book to my husband Jim for his faithfulness and courage to walk with me through a very long healing journey.

# Chapter 1

# Just Breathe

I felt his hand on the small of my back, gently guiding me through the crowded airport. "Just breathe" is what he said. What had caused me to come to this place? Why did I require coaching for the fundamentals of human existence? What was missing? What was wrong? Could the answer be traced to an experience that had been locked away decades before?

In a small, northern Alberta community, on September 21st, 1958, Allan and Tina held in their arms a blonde-haired, blue-eyed little girl named Teresa May. I was the third daughter, after the birth of their first-born son. My eyes sparkled with glee, as I faced the bright lights of the new world that I was about to discover.

Fourteen months later, another son arrived, to be followed by two sisters, who finished the clan. Seven children in eight years had made for a busy household, with many diapers and much work to do. Mom was kept running from early morning until the wee hours of the night, just to keep the house in order. The older siblings were part of the team who kept the clan together. With cows to milk and many mouths to feed, everyone chipped in as soon as they were able.

I responded quickly to the voices of my mother, father, and siblings. My bright smiles brought much joy to those around me. My older siblings thought that having this live doll to play with was a splendid idea. I looked forward to their antics and them dragging me around. The touch of people, and the kisses of my brothers and sisters, nurtured me, and made me smile. My hands reached out for more attention. My giggles made everyone soar. Hearing a person's voice would be all it would take for me to communicate, as only a little extroverted child could.

I toddled quickly to get to where I needed to go. I loved my family and all the activity about me. At the age of two, while deathly sick with bronchial pneumonia and in the hospital, I attached myself to the doctor and began calling him Daddy. The 104 degree fever made me lethargic and not responsive to my own mother, but still I reached out for the affections of the doctor. He responded with tenderness and pity, since I wasn't expected to live much longer. Although I was sick, those around me brought me much joy, and a peace that reassured me that it would be okay.

My mother worked hard to keep house and home going. I was thankful for my Grandpa Wiebe, who lived with us. He always had time for me, so I was with him as much as possible. He loved to have me on his lap, and would play with my ponytails. He rubbed my back, and touched my face tenderly. His gentle old hands would wipe away my tears when I would get hurt. He would let me sit by him for as long as I wanted. He cared so much for his little pumpkin. How I loved to be near him, and hear his voice calling me.

# Chapter 2

# The Black Spot

One morning, while still a toddler; I went to find him. I was disappointed to hear that he was sick in bed. With a sad heart, my first response was to go running into his room to be near him. He leaned over to put me on the bed, but he seemed rough today. It hurt when he pulled me up, and quickly tucked me under his protective arm beneath the covers.

Something was very different this morning. I said "ouch", but he didn't stop to hug it better. His gentleness was gone. He just pushed me under the covers, right near something very hard. His face was not kind, and he didn't smile at me. I had never seen him like this before. The pushing and pulling on my little body caused me to cry, but Grandpa pushed my face into his chest to muffle the sound.

I tried to get free, because it was hard to breathe, but he wouldn't stop. I didn't understand why Grandpa was hurting me. Once the hard thing was gone, he pulled me out from underneath the covers. He looked at me with eyes that were crying, and then placed his rough cheek next to mine and stroked my cheek—so gently—while whispering that he was sorry.

The man I knew and loved had returned. He wiped away the tears and told me how much he loved me. I wrapped my arms around his neck and knew that he hadn't meant to hurt me. I felt glad to have my old grandpa back—gentle and loving. Shortly after, he put me down on the floor and off I skipped to find the other kids so we could play.

The desire to play was there, but this time it was different. Everyone around me seemed to be the same, but I felt different. Why did my tummy hurt? I felt bad, like I had done something wrong. My feelings were different; it was like a black spot was in my tummy—a bad spot.

I felt like a bad girl, and like Mommy would be mad at me if she knew what had happened. When I played, I spoke louder and yelled more to mask the racing heartbeat. The kids kept telling me not to be so loud, or run so fast. But somehow, it made the feeling go away for a little while.

Activity was the name of the game in my household. If there were people involved, I was present. People seemed to make the loud beat of my heart quieter. When someone touched me I wanted more—to reassure myself of my value. I felt like I was always bad, or at least a little bad. Whether at work or play, I always wanted it to be fun and exciting. Fun and excitement took away the noise of the loud heartbeat. *Why do I feel so yucky? Does everyone else feel like this?* My little mind could not make sense of the emotions.

Mom would make cookies and while eating them it would all feel better. When they went inside of my body, they muffled the loudness of my heartbeat. They would soothe me, and calm my racing heart. Everyday it seemed to get a bit better, as long as there were a lot of people and activity—or at least some food. I always needed to silence that nagging heartbeat.

When the kids would not include me in a game, I would cry and the heartbeat would come back louder. Each time when I was hurt, and my mom or dad wasn't there, the black spot would grow a little more. *Does mommy care about my black spot? Do we all have one? I want the spot to go away*—I always felt less than the other kids. They played and didn't seem to be bad.

I loved Grandpa, and spent as much time as I could with him. But he seemed to be impatient with me, and did not let me sit up on his knee as much anymore. He wouldn't wipe away my tears like he used to, either. I missed his gentle old hand on my face. He used to slap his knee, encouraging me to jump up onto it, but that didn't happen anymore. "What did I do wrong?" I would mumble. He still wanted me to be around, but not as close as he used to.

Then, one day, he moved into his own little house in the yard, very close to our big white farmhouse. It was so exciting, for him and all of us. My mom had fixed it up and made it pretty. Grandpa was so happy, and wanted us all to see his new place. I was so happy. Grandpa would still be close, and I would be allowed to go see him whenever I wanted to.

It was a one-room house, with a bed, a propane stove, a wood heater, a table with two chairs, and a small corner cupboard where Grandpa kept his cookies. The ceiling above the table and the bed were yellow, because that's where he smoked. He would sit at the end of the table, facing the door, and play solitaire for hours and hours. When one of the children would come to the door, they were required to knock and wait for him to come or call out for us to come in. They would be allowed to sit and watch him play solitaire. It was rather still and boring in his little house. At times, he would have the radio playing quietly in the background.

I would often go to watch Grandpa as he played solitaire. He would talk to me once in awhile, but in general he would continue to play. One day, when I was about four, I entered the house and he invited me to sit on his knee. I was very excited, as I loved to be close to him. He laid the cards out, ready to begin another game. Then, suddenly, he became harsh and his breathing started to get heavy. He leaned his head heavily upon mine. I squirmed, because I was uncomfortable, but he just held me tighter and breathed harder. He pushed me tightly between his legs; it was hard to breathe and I wanted down.

When I started to cry, he hushed me up by putting his arm over my face. He squeezed hard, and there was something very hard pushing at me from behind. He began to push against my tummy with his hand, harder and harder until I felt like throwing up. I was crying and trying to move, but he just pushed me harder and faster. His whole body was tense and angry. *What did I do wrong?* I wondered.

It seemed to take so long. Finally, his whole body relaxed, and he let out a sigh of relief. Then he pushed me down off the chair. I stumbled and lay silently on the floor, looking up at him. My thoughts were only of why, and what I had done wrong to have Grandpa hurt me like that. I tried to approach him. I was sure he hadn't meant to hurt me, and wanted to say he was sorry, but instead he snapped at me and told me to go home, warning me not to tell anyone or I would be in big trouble.

I walked out of his house, and sat on the step, wondering what had gone wrong. He didn't say he was sorry for hurting me, and that made me feel so bad. The black spot got bigger that day, and the sound of my heart was louder. Then I quickly ran into the house to find someone to play with or

6

be with. It always felt better when someone was with me. I didn't know why I felt so bad, but I did.

I didn't like to go see Grandpa as he played solitaire anymore, but he would invite me to have a cookie—and make me sit up on his knee—many times. I was afraid not to obey him. It seemed to get worse all the time; he would push harder and demand more from me. I wanted him to say he was sorry and hug away the hurt. I just couldn't believe that Grandpa would be mean to me. I wanted to believe that all Grandpas were good and fun, and loved little children.

The visits seemed to be more and more frequent, and I wondered why he demanded that of me. With each visit, it became more and more clear that he would hurt me worse if I didn't come when asked, so I obeyed out of fear. His words— "This is all you are good for, and you're not worth anything more than shit!" —rang loud and clear in my little mind. Whenever I was asked where I had been, my response would be that I was just visiting Grandpa. He told me that if I spoke a word of it to my mom, he would get my two little sisters. I didn't want them to have to be hurt by him too, so I went each and every time I was called. Time passed, and I finally started school. What a relief! At least I wouldn't have to 'visit' Grandpa during school hours.

# Chapter 3

# Time Away

The time had come to start school and I was so excited. I would take lunch, ride the bus with the "big" kids, and go to grade one. There were lots of people there, and I loved to play with other kids. I was placed in Mrs. Sharkey's class, in the third desk from the front on the far left of the classroom. It was going to be a great year with Mrs. Sharkey. She was a lady from my church and her husband gave the kids peppermints every Sunday. As I looked around the room, I knew we were all going to be friends.

I was just feeling at home, and safe in my desk, when the principal of the school walked in. He announced that some of the children would have to go to Mrs. Patterson's classroom. I was certain that they would allow me to stay with Mrs. Sharkey, but my heart began to race as they approached my desk. I was told that I would have to leave the class. The tears flowed freely as Mrs. Sharkey led me down the hallway to the other classroom. While walking down the hall, the black spot seemed to grow bigger within me. Questions rang through my little mind: *What did I do wrong? Why did I have to move?* I came to the conclusion that I must be bad and that, somehow, I was being punished for it. Mrs. Patterson was a nice teacher, but I wanted to be with Mrs. Sharkey.

The year turned out to be pretty uneventful in terms of school, but my times with Grandpa were becoming a regular thing. It seemed that nobody cared what I wanted, so it didn't matter how much I hurt. When I would cry because it hurt, he wouldn't stop; he would hurt me more. Many times on the creaky, smelly floor of his house, I would cry out, but nobody came. He put whatever was handy—a stinky pillow, a pair of pants, socks, anything—on my face to muffle the sound.

I began to ask why, and his response was always given between heaving breaths. "This is all you're good for and you're worth nothing more than shit." Those words pierced my heart so deeply. When he would thrust himself deep within my tiny body, I would cry out and he would shove something into my mouth. The pain in my body was excruciating, but my heart hurt much worse. My heartbeat became so loud and strong that there were times I felt it would stop; that would have been my preference. *Why live, when all I'm worth is shit?* His words penetrated, so deep within my soul that I would smell my skin, because I thought I actually had a foul odor.

As time went on, he couldn't stand to see my face during the abuse—the one he loved became the one he hated. The child he had named, held, and cared for like none of the others, became the one he hurt, mistreated, and abused. My face became one of horror instead of love. He couldn't tolerate the look on my face, so he would cover it until I didn't fight him anymore. I would hold my breath until I couldn't feel the pain. I would go to a place within my mind that would protect me from his evil acts. He would perform his hideous deed and then kick me, to awaken me enough to get me out of his sight. I would scramble to get out as fast as I could, just to be away from him.

The black spot within my being became my life. I knew that I had no value or place of recognition in the family, so I set out to try to attain some. In grade two we had an award system in place for attendance, brushing our teeth, making our bed, reading, and so on. I won the prize, but only because I convinced the teacher that I actually did those things. I can't ever remember making my own bed or brushing my teeth before school. It felt so good, though, being praised in front of the class for how well I did in meeting the requirements of the contest.

I raced home to tell my siblings of my victory; they seemed jealous and that made me feel good. When presenting the award to my mom, I felt bad for having lied, but it felt good for the praise it brought. My heartbeat continued to go faster and faster, as I lied. I wanted more than anything to have the bad feeling within me go away. When people said kind things to me, it seemed to make me feel better—if only for a moment. Food would also make the pain seem less intense, but only while I was eating. There was one question I often asked myself: *Does everyone feel this way?*

Grandpa became ill and was no longer living on our yard. He had to go to the hospital—which was where he would stay until he died. As a 10-year-old girl, I smiled on the inside as dad took him away. My walk was light, and I hoped that he would never hurt me again.

I wanted the painful memories to be buried forever, but would they?

## Chapter 4

# Hope Flickers

I was told he had passed away. *I never have to remember this pain again—he's dead.* I smiled secretly to myself, as I walked lightly from the living room to the dining room. At age 10, I felt my life had just begun. With him out of the picture, I could laugh and play like any other child. With steely determination—on the day of his funeral, which I did not attend—I securely locked my pain-filled past away for good.

My heart raced, but this time the fear and pain were replaced with joy and excitement. From this day on, I decided that I would not remember what he had done to me. I quietly and quickly put it away, into a cavern deep within my being. It was dark, but I knew now that he was gone; he would never bother me again. The next day was school and I wouldn't feel bad anymore.

There was still, however, a desperate need for approval. Just like my parents at home, my teachers always seemed too busy for me. Some did manage to communicate affection to me, but even when I tried to do my best, I would still always feel like I hadn't quite done enough. There was a feeling of heaviness in my heart, but I was determined to ignore it. After all,

Grandpa was dead—I could now be a kid again. Little did I realize that what had happened would not come into the light until 20 years later.

Fortunately, I did have a number of women, besides my mother, who communicated to me that I had value: two aunts, a Sunday School Teacher, and my mom's friend. One day, for example, I hitchhiked to my aunt's house to 'get away from it all', but instead of feeling sorry for me, that aunt made me call my worried mom and take responsibility for my actions.

These ladies could see beyond the rebellion and hate. They seemed to love me no matter what. It was amazing how much I longed to be like them, and love people no matter what choices they made. To me, that was what God must be like. To the young me, those ladies were like "Jesus with skin on". They seemed to look beyond my faults and see my need.

Grade six was when my best friend's mom was killed in a car accident. It hurt so much to think that she no longer had a mom. I remember standing at the window, in the boot room at school, with her as the hearse drove by. No one talked to us about death then, or about how we felt. There was just silence. It seemed as though no one cared. We cried and held each other tightly, trying to find some comfort.

*Why did her dad have to drink, and her mom be killed? Doesn't anybody care?* The blackness in my soul seemed to get larger. I didn't want to think about that either, so I shared my mom with my friend. She spent many days and nights at our house, being treated as a family member. My dad cared more about her than he did me—at least that's how it felt. One night, as my friend lay crying, he gently sat beside her on the bed and comforted her. My jealousy grew as I watched his tenderness towards her. *Why doesn't he do that with me?*

The battle within me continued to rage. I always felt that I couldn't quite make the mark, so what was the point anyway. I didn't work as hard as my oldest sister, and didn't know how to cook and clean like my next sister, so what was the point of even trying. I knew there was something different about me. I only wanted to have fun, and play, and have people over. That didn't get the mouths fed or the work done. I felt I wasn't ever going to make anything of my life, so I might as well have fun.

The one positive place of rest and peace I found was Family Camp. The camp was surrounded in prayer and love. The director and his wife loved Jesus with all their hearts. I used to wish that I could be like her. She was pretty and could play the piano and organ beautifully. I knew that they were in love, because of the way they looked at each other. Her soft voice, and the tender tears that came to her eyes, made her a person I wanted to emulate. What they had was what I wanted for myself as well.

I knew, because of going to Sunday school and church all my life, that I needed a Savior. The black spot within my soul was getting larger and larger. *Could God take away my black spot?*

I knew Jesus came to set the captives free, and wash away our sins. I knew that when Jesus came, he died for the sins of the whole world, and that there was no way I would be able to go to heaven unless I surrendered my life to Him. One day at camp, when I was 12, I took the plunge and gave my life to Him. I prayed a simple prayer: "Dear Jesus; I am a sinner, I ask you to forgive my sin and change my life. I surrender the throne of my life to You and ask You to come and take control of me, in Jesus name, amen." I knew that Jesus had done just as I asked: He came in and took over the throne of my life.

When arriving home, I stood up at church to announced my new-found faith. I was so excited to be able to share the fact that I had come to this place in my life, and thought that everyone would be equally as excited. It didn't turn out that way. I felt rejected and unsupported in my new journey. That threw me for a loop. *Isn't this what everyone in church wanted for others?* I thought I had finally done what I was supposed to do, but it seemed they were just waiting for me to fall. And I did. I fell deeper than I, or anyone else, could have imagined. My heart became hardened. If God was judgmental and unloving, I didn't want any part of Him. Off I went, to find myself—my way.

## Chapter 5

# The Battle Rages

By age 13, I called myself an "official smoker". I was going to show "those people." The blackness within my soul was like a heavy weight that no one could explain. I knew that it was there, but didn't know its origin. *Does everyone feel like this?* I had thought that Jesus would take away all those yucky feelings of being worthless—valueless. Many times throughout my teenage life, I wished that I had the courage to kill myself. On occasion, the thought would monopolize my thinking, but somehow it would always vanish. I could not escape the desperation and negative feelings about myself. *How do I cope with this? Where do I turn? Does anybody know what to do about this darkness of my soul? If God doesn't care, why should I?*

Fun was a high priority in my life and, if there was none to be found, I would create it. By this time, my peers were the most important people in my life. The trouble with fun was that I didn't find too much of it in the right places. Church youth group and Sunday School class were okay, but somehow didn't cut it when trying to hush the loudly crashing waves of self-hatred in my mind. The words "too fat", "too dumb" and "not pretty" echoed loudly in my mind—so I lacked the three things that mattered most in my world.

I wasn't from a teacher's home or some family with a "name" in the community. I became the child who mothers told their adolescents not to hang out with, because I was a bad influence. Eventually, I stopped trying to convince them of anything different. After all, it didn't seem to matter how I felt or what needs I might have had. What people thought shouldn't matter to a "pile of shit", should it? After all, "shit" doesn't have feelings. Teens had a bad name anyway, and so I did my best to live up to it.

The only bright spots in my life were the times when I would go off to Family Camp each summer. There I was taken seriously—people actually listened to my ideas. Important people spoke to me. However, I was always very careful not to tell them about my true self. *If they knew me, they wouldn't like me either.* I thought that they would feel the same way about me that I felt about myself—that I thought everyone *else* thought about me: I was too moody, too loud, and too fat. I didn't see myself ever getting anywhere in life.

I recalled experiencing times of hope at Family Camp, whenever I would have a chance to love someone who I could tell didn't feel loved.

I sometimes traveled with a singer and his wife to another camp. It was an exciting time in my life, as I felt like God had somehow chosen me for a purpose. I worked hard at those camps, trying my best to please people. It was fulfilling and, at about the age of 14, I felt like God was calling me to be a pastor's wife, so that I could help people feel loved and accepted.

I loved how I could make people feel better, when I was able to hug them, talk to them, and listen to their hurts. Then I would pray and the person would feel better. God used me to bless people and help them face their problems. God knew that there was a better place for me. He placed the desire for it in my heart, long before I would ever desire to fulfill it. Each year, I would go home from camp and try to live differently, but very quickly would fall back into my old ways.

During my time at camp, an older man approached me in a sexual way. He told me nice things and touched me tenderly, so I was easily and quickly drawn into his approaches. He whispered kind words and, whenever he saw fit, would tell me to meet him in the woods for a walk. Then he would sexually use me for his own benefit.

I knew it was wrong, but he was a Christian and was being so kind to me so I convinced myself that it must be okay. Again, the darkness of my inner self grew larger. I knew I shouldn't be doing what I was doing, and felt very guilty, but could hardly wait until the next time. I was easy prey. Although I no longer understood why, or how, I felt that any value I had was all wrapped up in sex. The phrase, "this is all you are good for," echoed loudly through the chasm of my being. When I laid my head down on the pillow at night, I would plead with God to forgive me once again. I longed for freedom, but didn't even know what prison I was in.

Returning to school, and life at home, was always such a let down. At camp I felt some element of worth, but at home I didn't feel any at all. My heart would often break, desiring love and hope. *Does Jesus care? And if He does, why does it hurt so much?*

Junior High was an education of struggle, hate, rebellion, and pain (toward myself and others). The only brightness I found during this time was with some success in sports. Fortunately, I was athletic and loved to compete, so I did quite well. I played volleyball, fastball, and badminton. I used sports to get attention from my parents, and the few people who cared.

However, it didn't seem to matter how well I did. I never felt success like other people seemed to. I was too fat, too dumb, and certainly not pretty enough. I wanted to look like someone else, live somewhere else, and have someone else's brains. I thought that, if I had any one of those attributes, I would feel better and the black spot would be gone. The girls on my teams were either prettier, or better, or had a richer dad.

The one thing I wanted, more than anything, was to have my dad say how proud he was of me. I never felt I had lived up to his standards. During one volleyball tournament, Dad actually came to watch. I don't remember him being there any other time. I was so set on being the star player that I managed to sprain nearly all my fingers, but I didn't care. My daddy was watching.

When the coach offered me a break, I pleaded with him to let me play. The coach bandaged up my fingers and allowed me back on the court. Whenever I would hit the ball, I would look up to see Daddy's response. I saw none. He didn't want his daughter to get "puffed up", so no response was given. I yearned for my daddy's love and attention.

I knew he would be glad to have me play fastball. Again, I was hoping for a pat on the back. So, even though I was very young, off I went to join the team. It was dad's favorite sport. I was catcher, just like he had been. I thought this would bring the accolades I so desired. I tried my very best and worked my hardest, but came away from every game hearing my father's critical words: "You could have done …" "You missed that easy catch." Oh how my heart would hurt and yearn for Daddy to just wrap his arms around me and tell me

I was special and beautiful. His arms were never available, but there were always other men around who wanted me.

The guys enjoyed my antics and flirtatious moves. I knew how to attract them. I was well endowed long before my friends, and had always looked older than I was. I used it to get the much-needed attention. How I craved love and attention. I would fantasize about having a perfect relationship. The years passed with little regard for God or the morals that my mother had taught me. All I wanted was to feel good and feel loved. My lot in life was to live every day to its fullest and loudest so that this horrible feeling would go away.

After behaving so promiscuously with men, I knew for sure that my dream of living my life for God would never come to pass. I knew God would not have a purpose for me any longer—there were no secrets from Him. I might be able to fool a lot of people, but not God.

## Chapter 6

# A New Direction

*Could this be the night of my life?*

It was New Year's, 1976. I decided I was going to have the most fun ever, since this was my grade 12 year. I did manage to remember most of the night. The intoxication did not completely overcome me, but when finally arriving home the next day, it was more than just the horrible feeling of having smoked my brains out that made me sick. It was the vacancy of love in my heart. I wanted to die.

I tried so hard to think of what would make me feel better—but I didn't know what was making things hurt so much. It wasn't what anybody had done or said. It was like a cloud had rolled in and I'd found myself in the middle of it with nowhere to run. The longing in my soul was crying loudly. It had no voice to say what it needed, just a longing for release—a longing for freedom.

In desperation, I cried out to God. I knew from all my Sunday School days, and my mom's teaching, that God was alive, and that He promised life. But how could I approach Him after all I had done? How could I dare to ask for help, let alone love? Would He care to listen to my plea? Oh well, it didn't matter anyway. I threw myself before Him. I cried, and begged, and pleaded for Him to show Himself to me in some small way. I needed to know He was there. I needed to know He was listening, so I asked Him to show me.

At that moment, there was a sense of a presence in the room. A calmness began to roll over my heart. I knew that God was there, but how could I dare ask for forgiveness for all I had done? If I did, what would He require of me? I began by telling Him all my feelings of regret, especially for my promiscuous lifestyle. I felt unclean and bare—raw—without any protection. But when I had laid it out, a peace began to flood over me. The weight of all my wrong choices began to seem lighter. Then I asked Him if He would make me feel like a girl again, rather than the whore I saw in the mirror. The impurity of my being seemed to speak louder than any voice, so I gave Him all of my filth.

The cigarettes on the dresser felt like a big barrier between us, so I asked that He take away the desire to ever smoke again. *Why should God care about such an unclean, unworthy girl who has made so many wrong decisions?* I believed I didn't deserve anything, but I hoped He would believe in me anyway. If not, I wanted Him to stop my heart that night. I knew He had the power to do that. Death would be better than continuing to live the way I had been.

After laying it all down at Jesus' feet, I slept. The peace that flooded my being that night was unexplainable. I didn't care if God stopped my heart, because it was His again. I felt that He might somehow have a purpose for me. It was so wonderful to sleep in peace, knowing I was forgiven. The darkness seemed to be veiled and separated from my mind. The loudness in my soul was quieted. *God is good! He did care for me and had a plan for my life.*

The next day was Sunday. When Mom called to see if I wanted to go to church, I was up in a flash and ready to go. Mom concealed her astonishment and just did the regular Sunday morning things. After church, I went and confirmed my commitment with Pastor Larry Haugan. He expressed his joy and prayed with me. Even the people in the church seemed different that day. It didn't matter whether or not they accepted me. I knew I had peace in my heart.

On the drive home, I asked Mom if she noticed anything different about me. Mom choked up quickly. "Did I notice?" She was thrilled to see my new desire to follow Christ in a big way, but was wary of how long it would last. I was known for my rash decisions and it seemed that it was in my nature to do things for as long as it was convenient. This time was different. I didn't care how much people doubted my commitment. I knew I had a peace that no one could take away.

Within three weeks, I was in Bible College. The school community was a great support for my new faith walk. It was a miraculous turn of events in my life, to be able to be in such safe surroundings. The students there accepted and included me immediately. People there were growing in Christ, and wanting to be more like Him. My sister was there, and she played a big role in helping me feel included. Soon, I was involved in singing in the choir and loving it.

I loved my classes with Mr. McNair. He was a nice man. He spoke gently and kindly, and with a touch of sarcasm. The Dean of Women was a very special lady, who listened well and prayed with me. I felt accepted by her. It wasn't long before I had established deep friendships with the girls in my dorm. The boys seemed awfully nice too, and I was certainly open to finding one I might like to marry. After hanging out with a couple of guys, I soon realized that I was not ready for that. I needed to grow in Christ and ask His permission and learn His will concerning that area of my life.

The ministry seemed to be calling my name. I felt I would love to be a pastor's wife, but how could someone with my background qualify? *Is it possible this is from God? I think it may have been possible, before I made all those wrong decisions, but not now."* There was no way God could be calling me, but I surrendered the decision to Him. God can make anything possible if we are available and open to Him. "He will make us able" are the words I heard in class. My response, thinking there was no way He would call me considering my trashy past, was simple: "Yes God."

Meanwhile, I was going to enjoy my time at Bible School and doing the thing I loved to do—sing. The choir director and his wife were genuine people, who loved God and loved their students. They had such an amazing way of helping me feel accepted and cared for. When on tour with the choir, I felt safe and secure with them.

I began to pray for a God-fearing man to have for my husband. I would bow beside my bed whenever the longing for a man's arms would take my focus off of why God had brought me there. I would spend much time in prayer, asking God to remove the longing I was feeling and change it to something else that He would like and want for me. I yearned to please God and become more like Christ. The most important trait I wanted in a man was the desire to please God and the ability to forgive me for my past.

Jim and his best friend were the spiritual giants of the school—at least from my perspective. By my standards, they were not exactly catches—spiritually yes, but they were too serious about everything. Yet, they had caught my eye, and something seemed to draw me to them. Jim was a mystery and a challenge, because he was so committed to his studies that he certainly had no interest in girls. They were obviously the last thing on his mind. His clothing was outdated, and it didn't seem to bother him a bit. He was there to study and do the will of God; that was all that mattered to him.

However, God had other plans that neither of us realized. I might have run had I known, and he would have for sure. He was considering becoming a pastor and didn't want a woman getting in the way. The Lord prompted Jim to show acceptance and sisterly love toward this little blonde girl named Teresa Wiebe. Little did either of us realize where it would lead! During our talks in the library and walks outside, he relayed to me his desire to follow God wherever He would lead. I loved his devotion for God, and wanted to learn all I could from him. My feelings for him, began to show up quicker than I thought possible. Jim didn't want any feelings, so wouldn't allow them to surface, but we both sensed the Lord encouraging us to grow in love with each other for the next year and a half.

Soon it was time for Jim to graduate. He planned to go to England for another year of Bible School training. He seemed to care deeply about me, but I still had not disclosed my past life to him. Twenty minutes from campus, while sitting at A & W drive-in, I told him that I was not a virgin. I gave him room to run, to escape from the relationship, but his words still echo in my ears today. They were words of love and acceptance.

"Do you have a child?"

"And if I do?" I asked, curious to see how he would respond.

"If you do, and if it's God's will for us to be married, then I guess I'll be a dad."

That was his gracious reply, and I wondered how that could be true.

God's will was far more important to him than anything else. It was never even mentioned how such a thing would affect his reputation or how it would look to the ministry. He never asked how could I do such a thing. It was love—God's unconditional love.

*"Therefore, there is now no condemnation for those who are in Christ Jesus."(Romans 8:1 NIV).*

We were engaged in July 1977, and on my 19th birthday he flew off to England for a year of studies. The tears flowed, feelings of abandonment set in, and doubts about how he could possibly love me monopolized my thoughts. Jim experienced many times of doubt and fear himself, of whether or not he could possibly be my husband. He decided to come home for Christmas and his doing so seemed to cement, in both of us, the need my fragile heart had for security. He was the kind of guy I needed.

What a great man of God I was going to marry! He came home after completing his year, with many stories to tell of Ireland's police service, the difficulty in interpreting the different English dialects, and how he grew in his faith—experiencing God in amazing ways.

August 12th, 1978 was the big day, my wedding. The wedding rehearsal had gone perfectly. We had a rehearsal dinner at the Golden Star in Grande Prairie, Alberta—to celebrate our upcoming marriage and my Parents 25th wedding anniversary. It all went off without a hitch.

The tables and chairs were all set up in the back yard for the outdoor reception, which would be held immediately following the ceremony. After 21 days of beautiful sunshine I was anticipating day number 22 to be the best, most perfect one ever. After all, I was getting married that day. I could see it all in plain view—the decorated cars bringing me and my new husband out to the farm, to celebrate what the Lord had brought together. I trusted Him to bring about my wishes. I went to sleep the night before in great anticipation of being the bride.

Morning came, and the sun was not shining through the window in my bedroom. I quickly got up, looked out, and found that it was pouring rain. It was dark and bleak outside, and my first thought was, *I don't deserve a nice beautiful day for my wedding, do I?*

I could hear a lot of scurrying around downstairs. My mom had prepared and put all the food in the basement, and now had to somehow figure out what needed to be done. What were we going to do with the over 200 people coming to the reception?

The day had many ups and downs, but in the end Jim and I were married, and off to our honeymoon suite in Grande Prairie, and wedded bliss—or so we thought.

Jim had stopped in beforehand to confirm the reservation, and offered to pay for the room ahead of time, but they promised to keep it for us without a deposit. However, when we arrived, the honeymoon suite had been rented out to someone else, and the newlyweds ended up in the Sandman Inn for our first night together. It didn't matter though, because being married to such a caring and loving man was all I needed to make everything right.

On our three week honeymoon, we discovered we were very different. I was extremely extroverted and tended to nag, and he was introverted and would climb into his "cave", which would frustrate me and prompt me to "extrovert" all over him—on and on the cycle would go. Somehow things weren't perfect but I knew it would be wedded bliss once we were settled. That's how it is for everyone, isn't it? After going to help Jim's uncle with the harvest in September, we moved to Kitimat, BC, where Jim was offered a job at the Alliance Church as assistant/youth pastor.

This was where God had led us, and being a pastor's wife would change everything. Or would it?

# Chapter 7

# "Bliss" – at last?

I knew God had called us into ministry; we were both convinced of our calling. It didn't take long before we were in the groove of it. I soon realized that Jim's love and call to ministry were first and foremost in his mind. Nothing, including me, seemed to matter, or factor into his equation. I became extremely lonely and wished I could get his attention.

I became very involved in the church as well. There were outbursts between us, where I would accuse him of loving the church more than me. I would become violent, and hurt him by yelling and using inappropriate language to display intensity. How I longed for a man who would see me as his only priority, to whom he would dedicate all his time and attention. I knew that, if he would do that for me, my life would be better.

Shortly after we moved to Kitimat, BC I received a phone call informing me that my uncle had passed away. He was 49 years old and had died of a heart attack. I wanted so much to be able to go home, but there was no money to be spared for the trip. Three weeks later, I found myself packing up and leaving to attend my own father's funeral. Missing that was simply not an option.

The devastation of loss, and the fear of more death, overcame me as we began our journey home in the pouring rain. The rain turned to snow and, just about an hour from Kitimat, we rolled our van. In the ditch, with Jim knocked out and laying across me, I thought, *"Now what do I do?"* There we were, many miles from home, in an incredible storm; Jim was hurt, and I needed to get home for my Dad's funeral. Fortunately, the windshield popped out so I was able to climb through the opening. Jim came to and discovered I was up on the highway hailing a semi which took us back to Terrace.

Fortunately, we had no serious injuries. After being checked over in the hospital, we ended up staying the night with friends of friends. We helped them bail out the basement entry, as the storm continued to rage. It turned out to be the unforgettable "Terrace-Kitimat flood of 1978".

Eventually, we arrived home to attend my father's funeral. There, I wrestled with the fact that I had never heard him say "I love you," and now never would, and the painful array of emotions that caused. Before long, I was back on the road to Kitimat, where life would be different.

It was lonely there, but at least I didn't have to deal with his death. At a church event, a lady from the community whispered "You don't have to be a hero here." Those words broke the dam that had built up inside me. I was hurting so desperately, because my dad had not voiced those three most important words to me. I thought he probably did love me; he *had* provided for us, and in the last couple of years, he seemed to be more responsive.

I had apologized to him for hating him so much and it had helped, but he still didn't have the freedom of emotion to express his love to me. I yearned for my daddy's love, to be clear in his actions and his words. But now that opportunity was gone forever, and so I quietly tucked it into the bank of pain I had accumulated over the years, where the other hurts lay dormant, and festering.

I went full-force back into our life of ministry, trying to figure out what it really looked like for Jim and me. I knew he loved and had a passion for what he was doing, and that somehow I would need to fit myself into that part of him. But how would that look? I went before God and sought out understanding of His plan for my life. How could I be the best wife Jim could ever imagine? I wanted the best for us—not some mediocre marriage *or* ministry. My prayer, to become the best wife Jim could have, began a journey of discovery, on which I learned what God really wanted for me. I loved the life of ministry, and certainly didn't mind the upfront, interactive part of it. I loved being called on to help people, finding out what they needed and lending my assistance in any way I could. I felt hopeful that, maybe, I would find my life's purpose, given to me by God, in ministry.

Four months after arriving in Kitimat, it was discovered that I had an ovarian cyst. After many trips to doctors and specialists, they basically found out that I had a messed-up abdomen. I felt discouraged and wondered if God would ever allow me to be a mom. The doctors explained that having a child of my own would be impossible until I had a uterine suspension, and even then there was no guarantee. Thus began a series of hospital stays, which included three surgeries.

As much as I longed to be a mother, when I was honest with myself, I felt that I was unworthy to have such a privilege.—*"You're not worth anymore than shit and this is all you're good for"*—so I quickly put it out of my mind. My obligation was to keep Jim happy, and it was not my place to ask for the rest. My value was not that important anyway, so I went on my way, trying to make something of my life. If doing that meant ignoring myself, to the point of exhaustion, then that is what I would do. After all, was that not what Christ required of me, to lay down my life for others? I was more than willing to do that. I knew that, eventually, I would sense some value in myself, because I was obeying the commands of Scripture.

I set out to do all I could for Christ: teaching at a private school, helping with worship, leading choirs, singing, and so on. My limitations were not a factor in the equation. I lived only to serve. How else could I expect to have any significance in life? In that sacrifice, I had given up on having the marriage I thought, and hoped, would be mine. Jim was so busy serving God that he forgot about me at home. He was scheduled every day, and every night, and I started to wonder if I would even be missed if I weren't there. Those feelings of worthlessness were confirmed once again.

The chasm of loneliness began to set in. "*Who cares about me anyway?*" Only God knew the pain of my heart, and I felt that He wasn't listening. If He was, then why wouldn't He change it? I would cry out to Him, in desperation for my marriage and my own self-worth. "*Does Jesus care about me?*" These were the words that echoed loudly within my soul. How desperately I needed a ray of hope in my life.

A visiting Christian teacher came to our church and challenged people to embrace having a life purpose. He helped Jim to see why he had been created and how to apply that reason to his life. He needed to have his priorities rearranged, and from then on, I was to be number one—after his relationship with Jesus. I was to be included in his daily life, and not just whenever he happened to have time left over.

It really helped me to see that God answers prayer, and that I was being heard. As our life began to grow together, and Jim spent more time with me, I felt like I finally had some value in his eyes and my faith soared. I had the faith to believe that I could actually be of use to God, in many ways.

I started journaling my prayers, and it seemed to help me to write down the words my heart was crying out. This was it; I now felt that I had finally found the key to adding value to my life. Oh, how I longed to be an awesome pastor's wife! How I loved the positive attention, but certainly not the painful. I was amazed that God could use me, with my trashy background, in his church. *"Wow!"* I thought. *"Only God could use me in this way, because I know I am inadequate."*

After my final surgery, the doctor said I was good to go. He did not give me any guarantee, regarding children, but said that at least everything was put back in its correct place. It should take away all the pain I had been living with, and I should experience a time of healing for my body. I was excited about the possibility of feeling better. That last surgery was in March and, the following June, Jim and I moved to Quesnel, BC.

A new adventure was always a time of anticipation in my life. This would give us a new start—one in which I was feeling better and would try to be the perfect pastor's wife. God had prepared us for this new challenge, the establishment or "planting" of a new church. *"Wow, how do we even do that?"* It seemed important, and doable, but cash flow was very slim. Money seemed to always be a factor in my life. I wanted more, and felt somewhat cheated in the ministry. It didn't matter how many hours or how hard we worked, the cash flow never increased.

The demands on our time and place of residence were unbelievable, because our way of church planting was to have lots of people in our home. How I longed for enough money to make ends meet, and maybe even some luxury, which would give me value. *"Oh well, I know I'm not worth anything anyway, so I guess it's irrelevant."* Everything in life seemed to end the same: with me having no say in the grand scheme of things. But I hoped that the harder I worked and the more I sacrificed, the more the ugliness would fade away. I yearned for that peace of heart and mind that would come with knowing that God actually had a purpose in mind for me, not just an existence.

Was this the abundant life of which Jesus spoke in the Bible?

# Chapter 8

# "ME" – A MOM!!!

I thought I must be imagining it …

Shortly after moving to Quesnel, I began to feel sick to my stomach. *"No,"* I thought, *"I can't be pregnant could I? God wouldn't grant us children, would He?"* I knew I didn't deserve to be a mother and—even if I truly was being given this gift—I knew that I would probably be a very poor one.

As it turns out, I *was* pregnant, with little Jonathan Allan Thomas, who would become our first son.

The anticipation of this little one brought much joy and meaning to my life. I would sing to my growing abdomen, and pray that this child would live to serve Jesus with his whole heart. My desire was to have a godly family, one who experienced His wholeness and grace. I longed to hold this little one in my arms; my arms ached at the thought of not being able to embrace him.

On February 23, 1981, at 3:50 in the afternoon, Jonathan lay cooing in his mother's arms. *"Could this be? A child who will call me mom? – I am it. I am solely responsible to nurture this little gift from God!* "Oh God!" I cried, "I want to be the best mom this little child could ever dream of!"

I wanted him to know that he was so important the world would stop if he wasn't in it. I prayed for Jonathan to be all that God had in mind for him. As God wove him together in my womb, I desired him to be a disciple of Jesus.

I loved being his mom. Often the feelings of worthlessness would creep back in, trying to rob me of my joy, but I wanted him to know how important he was so I pushed those feelings aside. Jonathan was a very responsive little baby. I spent hours singing to him, and taking him for walks. It seemed to give me some sense of worth and value. Even if I would always fall short, at least now I was training a child to really become what God intended. My biggest desire was that he would always know his value.

While trying to adjust to my new role as mother, I still had to keep up my responsibilities at the church. I believed that was where God wanted me to be, and felt that there was no such thing as taking a break. It was, after all, what gave my life meaning and purpose. I did nursery shifts, and taught Sunday School, and played the piano for service. Wasn't that my place—in the service of God? Didn't God expect me to keep up my tasks? How could I possibly expect others to do things, if I wasn't doing them too? And besides, doing all that I could to serve God was what helped me feel to better about myself.

Jonathan was just 5 months old when the nausea returned, and I discovered that I was pregnant again. Jennifer Teresa May was being knit together inside me. When visiting the doctor to have my pregnancy confirmed, he suggested that I should terminate it—in view of my physical situation. I was appalled at the thought; first of all, it was wrong, and secondly, I might never have the chance again.

I pleaded before God once again, praying that this little one would live for Jesus, or that he would just go ahead and take her to be with Him now. I really didn't want any child who wouldn't live for Jesus. It would be hard enough being a parent; if I had children who would not be open to God it would be that much harder. Too hard.

I often cried out to Him on their behalf. How I longed for a warm, loving, caring, godly home, and family—one that people would recognize as being so. My desire was never to be normal or mediocre. I wanted an above-average family, whose simple existence truly glorified God.

Jennifer arrived on May 11, 1982, with beautiful pink cheeks, and all ten fingers and toes. Her name means "Our fair lady" and that is what she was from the day she was born. "*Wow, how did I rate getting to have a boy and a girl?*" I felt so unworthy, to have gotten what I wanted. I knew I didn't deserve it, but I thanked God and promised Him that I would try my very best to be all He wanted me to be as their mother.

I always felt that, as a real disciple of Christ, I should be doing more, and enjoying life less. While our children were young, I had a sense of peace just spending time with them, but there was also so much to do in the church. How could I manage both, without either one feeling neglected?

I set my heart straight to the task of undertaking all of the above. I didn't want my kids to feel neglected in any way, so I would work constantly on both. Visiting and spending time with people was my love, so I would haul the kids around everywhere. They slept under chairs at meetings, and in other people's bedrooms when I was counseling. They became adaptable at sleeping and playing with anyone, anywhere. Jonathan and Jennifer were each other's best friends, and loved to play together. How precious they were! The delight they brought to my heart was great, as I watched them grow up. How had I grown up?

# Chapter 9

# Questioning the Past

Seeing how Jim related to Jennifer made me question my past. Watching them caused me to realize that children were allowed to make mistakes and still feel loved and accepted. Furthermore, they were to be treasured and valued. It was a picture of God's love for me.

The privilege and responsibility of being a mom revealed to me a need to live in complete dependence on the Holy Spirit. I would cry out to Him, knowing that He knew our children's needs better than I did. I struggled with fear, thinking that they may be taken from me—after all, isn't that what I deserved. I continued to surrender them to God, and pray that they would follow Jesus, no matter what. I had heard that fasting and prayer was effective, so throughout their lives I fasted and prayed for them.

After living in Quesnel for five years, we knew it was time for us to move on. Jim had a dream of going overseas, which meant pursuing more education. First, we went to Edmonton, Alberta, where I had a complete hysterectomy, because the doctor had explained that my abdomen was in a pre-cancerous stage.

I got a severe infection, and it took a whole year before I lived without constant pain. Shortly after that, we moved to Regina, Saskatchewan, where Jim completed his master's degree in divinity, and I finished two years of Bible School training.

Every semester, the Seminary and College organized a Spiritual Emphasis Week. One time, a speaker spoke to us about the need to live free in Christ. He described spiritual bondage, a lack of carry through, self-hatred, private sins, outbursts of rage for no apparent reason … there were dedicated Christians wanting to follow Christ, but always being hindered by one thing or another. He spoke about feeling a prisoner in your own body, without the freedom to get beyond a certain point because of past experiences. As he spoke, it was as though he were telling my own story of bondage, and it became painfully clear that he was talking *to* me—*about* me.

After the session, I told Jim that I really needed to go see the man, but wouldn't go without him holding my hand. So we made the appointment, and it was revealed to us, through prayer, that I had an evil spirit residing in my right side. The amazing part for us was that I knew exactly where it was, and its color. That day, as I prayed for it, I physically felt the evil presence, the black spot, leave. Jesus had set me free, and was then able to begin His real work of healing in my life. It was then that the layers of hurt and self-judgment began to fall away. When we made the move to Whitecourt, AB for another church plant, we had no idea what God had in store for us.

# Chapter 10

# The Healing Journey

It was 6:00 am, when I was awakened by a dream. I felt help-less knowing the little child, who had been being sexually abused, was me. After writing down all that I had seen, I called my friend Deb. She rushed over and knelt beside my bed as I read the horror to her. I will never forget her words to me: "I believe you." She reached out her arms and held me close. As we cried together, all she said was, "I'm sorry and I'm here."

It was the beginning of a long emotional journey together. She listened; I cried; she cared; I was angry; she didn't condemn. There are no words to describe those moments together, or what they meant to me.

Jim had gone hunting early that morning. When he arrived home, Deb left (after caring for our kids). Then I read my journal writings to him. Instead of condemnation, he was angry, *but not at me*.

At last, that little girl felt as though a man was there to defend her. His words meant so much: "Oh Babe, if he were alive, I would want to kill him." It felt so good to hear those words. He was a defender of the weak—and oh how weak I was. My mind didn't know where to go. It was in that moment that I heard the words, "Just breathe". That was all I needed to do: breathe in, and let it go. That has been the counsel I have shared with others, but also with myself whenever life's circumstances overwhelm me.

Many exercises have helped me in my healing journey. Through the time I spent rehashing the feelings, and the desperation, I clung tightly to the Word of God.

I found some life-giving promises: Luke 4:18, where Jesus said that He came to set the captives free; and John 8:32, which says that those He sets free are free indeed.

Oh how I wanted freedom—freedom from the chains that strangled me, freedom from the voices of my past, freedom from the chasm of self-doubt and self-hatred.

The Psalms speak deep into the heart of all of us. In them, David has penned our heart's needs and longings. If you were to leaf through my Bible, page 707 would stand out in your mind.

At the top of the page, are the words. "FAVORITE PSALM." There are many handwritten notes in the margin of Psalm 139, because it's a psalm that I have often turned to: when wondering if my personality was a mistake; when I missed my kids because they were in some other country; when feeling like God had somehow become missing in action. It reminds me that I was knit together in my mother's womb—exactly the way the designer planned—and that, "ALL the days ordained for me were written in [God's] book before one of them came to be". I echoed David's words in my heart and mind: "How precious to me are your thoughts, O God!"

One of the entries in my journal, from March 1990, captured the pain I was in for much of my life: "The pain is so painful I can hardly bear it. You really care don't you? It hurts so much; my whole body is aching. I want to love and be loved. My whole life seems confused."

I spent many hours—and still do—communicating with God regarding my pain, and the questions I had. There are no secrets with Him. He wants us to tell Him everything, for our sake, and I found that writing them down was one of the most helpful ways. It has enabled me to say "hello" and then "goodbye" to my pain. But best of all, it's helped me to embrace the amazing grace of God. When you think about it, the Psalms are really David's journals.

I was greatly helped by a number of books I have read: *Freeing Your Mind from Memories That Bind,* by Fred & Florence Littauer; and *Love Hunger,* by Frank Minirth; as well as several others. Through them, I was able to put more of my questions into words.

In my journey of healing, I also traveled an hour and a half from our home to receive counseling, from a man who loved God and desired for people to live in freedom. He would let me talk about whatever I needed. One day, as I began my drive home, I realized that I was emotionally exhausted. Part way down Highway 43, I pulled into a campsite, laid my seat back, and fell asleep. Shortly after nodding off, I began to dream.

A little baby was flailing in her bassinet, and no one could console her.

I was standing at the end of a long hallway listening, and Jesus was right beside me. I looked at Him and asked, "What's wrong with that baby?"

"She doesn't know she's wanted," He said.

"Well, is she?" was my response. "More than she will ever know," He said. "I have plans for her—to prosper her and not harm her, to give her a future and a hope" I recognized His words from Jeremiah 29:11.

"Let's go tell her," I said with excitement. "After you," He said.

We walked down the hallway together. He never pushed once; every time I hesitated, He just waited. He is a perfect gentleman.

Upon reaching the frantic child, I realized that she was me. My thoughts raced: *"Why was I born? Why did God allow me to be conceived, if all I was good for was poop and sex?"*

No one could console me, but Him. As He gently caressed my little head, and spoke quietly in my ear, I began to calm. He spoke tenderly. "I love you my sweet baby, and know each day this heart will beat. Be still my little one," Then He consoled me with Joshua 1:5: "I will never leave you nor forsake you."

As the baby's tears dried, my heart was overwhelmed with how much I had needed to know that Jesus hadn't fallen asleep during the pain—that He was there all the time. He felt each kick. Each and every day that I would hold my breath, He was there. He was present—He was with me. We stayed there in that room for awhile, as I reveled in the joy of knowing I was planned, and not just an accident to be hurt and abused. I was completely planned, and woven together in my mother's womb, for a purpose: to know God and love Him forever.

When we turned to leave the room, I realized that the hall Jesus and I had walked down had many doors. It was the corridor of my life. We opened a few of them, and looked inside. Each held good memories: skating on the rink in our back yard; harvesting the garden in the fall; driving the tractor with my little brother; Saturday night baths; and family meals, with dad at the head of the table and the other eight of us completing the circle. Milking cows early in the morning, running down the lane to catch the bus, mowing the lawn, watching soap operas while shelling peas, arguing over chores, and many other times spent with family and friends came to mind.

One of the doors had been locked from the inside, and there were old rough boards nailed across it. No one was getting into that one. I looked at Jesus and wondered what was in there. "The information behind that door is painful," He whispered, so gently. When I asked Him if it was *my* pain, He nodded His head, and cried.

I wasn't sure I wanted to go there, but my longing for freedom from the past, and Jesus' offer to never leave me, began the journey of hope, hope beyond the hurt. Jesus never once pushed me. He waited for me to ask, and then gave me the strength to remove each board that I couldn't get off on my own. When all the bars were gone, He unlocked the door to what was inside.

My first thought was to wonder, if my grandpa would be able to go back there with me, if he were alive ... and if he admitted what he had done, and asked for my forgiveness, would that take away the pain and scars? What if my mom or dad could go back there? I could share with them the reality of the abuse. Would that take away the hurt

No.

There was only *one* who could accompany me to visit the pain; there was only *one* who could walk with me, through the losses and emotional hurt, and He did! The Timeless One, the All-Knowing/Understanding One—Jesus.

That day, I surrendered my journey into the hands of the One being able to do exceedingly, abundantly more than we could ever ask or imagine. That was the day I discovered the depths of my abuse. It took me down the road toward embracing and releasing the pain, and no one on this earth could meet me there, but Jesus did!

As I awoke from the dream, my heart began to sing because I knew two very important facts: I wasn't an accident only here to be abused; and Jesus wasn't going anywhere—He was in it, the healing, for the long haul.

He had come to set me free, and when He does that, *we are free indeed!*

# Chapter 11

# "Forgive Him?"

"Don't forgive too soon" was what one of my counsellors' recommended. It was helpful advice, but confusing and difficult.

Early on in my healing journey, I realized the need to forgive. It was much easier said than done. The whole arena of forgiveness seemed to be a "tug of war" between my mind/will and my feelings. As Christ's follower, I knew I had to forgive, but could I really find it in my heart to do so? I also knew that to do the opposite was dangerous. I had heard it said that not forgiving is like drinking poison and hoping the other person dies. I had a lot of poison in me that I needed to get rid of. Why live and die a bitter person?

Probably the best way to describe it is this: I made one big choice, by the act of my will, to forgive my grandfather. Unforgiving feelings often surfaced after that. Each time, I would revisit the emotional, physical, or social loss, and choose to release it also. It was very difficult, but helpful.

I still remember going alone to visit my grandfather's grave. It was an overcast day, with gently falling rain. Through my tears, I told my grandfather of all the losses I had suffered at his hands: the loss of my childhood; the ability to think like a child, dream like a child, and hope with childlike faith.

It seemed to me that God too was crying, as the rain fell. I left that graveyard greatly released in spirit. Since that day, when pangs of loss and unforgiveness hit me, I continue to revisit and release them. You have to say "hello" to the pain before you can freely say "good-bye"—and then I make a further choice to continue in forgiveness. Owning my emotions has helped me walk in freedom.

I would never be able to live this freely, without knowing our heavenly Father. Understanding something of His attributes has propelled me forward in this experience. Glimpsing the absolute grandeur of His being has caused me to humble myself before Him.

Understanding something of His holiness and utter purity has caused me to see my personal sinfulness and separation from Him. Discovering the abuse Christ went through for my sins, and the sins of the whole world, has been totally humbling. Accepting that Christ has fully forgiven all my sinfulness, and brought me into His Presence, has been life transforming. Living in the reality of such grace has brought love, joy, peace, and hope.

It has also helped me to realize that I, too, must extend that forgiveness to those who have offended me—not least of all my grandfather. Indeed, the ground is level at the foot of the cross. It does not matter who we are or what we have done. Jesus alone can show us the way to experience the grace of our Father, and to pass it on.

# Chapter 12

# My "Mat Carriers"

I love the story in Mark 2:1-12, about a paralytic. It describes how four men carried him to Jesus and he was healed. They carried him to the only One who is able to heal completely, from the inside out. Jesus said to him, "…your sins are forgiven … get up, take your mat and walk".

I was paralyzed by fear, anger, and bitterness. I needed people to pray that I would be able to break through the ceiling of pain, and carry me to the One who could forgive sins and heal the wounds in my heart. I needed people to journey with me.

I have been blessed throughout my life, with many people who have helped lead me to Jesus, and brought me to where I am today.

Some listened.

Some cared.

Some don't even know how their actions and words drew me to Him.

We belonged to a small group with whom I could share my journey. They, and my precious sister—who lived in the same town as we did at that time—were there for us all the way.

I am thankful to have had a praying, godly mom. When she heard the story of what had happened to me as a child, her heart broke and she asked my forgiveness for not protecting me. She continues to carry me to Jesus.

I am grateful to my husband, who has hung in there through "thick and thin". I feared, most days, that he would eventually be done with the process—that he would just simply pack up and move on. I assumed that he would leave.

One morning, I awoke in tears, again, thinking for sure that this would be the day. But when he understood my upset, he took my face into his hands and affirmed our marriage covenant: that if this marriage were to ever end, he would not be the one leaving.

"I love you," he said, "and am not going anywhere … ever."

I fell into his arms and wept, telling him that I would need to hear that again and again.

A day never goes by, even now—over 20 years later—without me *knowing* I am loved and that he will be here till death do us part or Jesus returns.

My kids have taught me what it is to be a child, and have grown up into responsible, loving adults. They, without knowing it, were the channel God used to show me how a Father loves his children. I remember watching as Jim tenderly hugged them and encouraged them before they headed off to school. "You are amazing kids and don't let anybody tell you any different," he would say, or remind them that their backpacks were full of Jesus.

His unwavering, steady presence in their lives showed me the way God loves us. Their innocence, childlike faith, and confidence in me as their mom helped me grow in my self-worth. Now, as adults, their continuing support and prayers are with me as I travel, and tell my story. My heart is over-whelmed with gratitude for each of them, and their spouses, for their friendship and blessing in my life. They have been my "mat carriers" in the truest sense of the word.

There have been times, after those first four years of intense healing, that God has revealed Himself to me in surprising ways. I have asked Him to change some of the horrible "pictures"—images, and sensory memories from my past. The worst one was of the stench of dung. When crying out to God one day, for a new picture, it came to me very clearly, in the form of a question: "What makes a garden most productive or flowers so beautiful?" The answer? That's right. Dung! Ecclesiastes 3:11(NIV) says: "He makes everything beautiful in its time".

Jesus gives beauty for ashes. He not only forgives and heals, but redeems—causes the flowers to bloom. If I were to choose to be a flower it would be a daffodil, because when they bloom, they look up to heaven and smile—praising God for all He has done.

# Epilogue

Today, Jim and I continue to live in God's healing grace. We have been blessed to have a third child, Nicole, adopt us as parents. All three of our children have married terrific followers of Christ. They have made us the proud grandparents of eleven.

Today, my story of "*Hope Beyond Hurt*" continues to resonate with many people around the world. God's desire is to heal all of us—from the inside out. It doesn't matter how deep the pain, Jesus can go there and redeem what has been lost, or stolen.

How about you? What unresolved pain lingers in you? Do you know hope beyond hurt? Would you like to?

# Appendix 1

## Helps for Hope Beyond Hurt:

1. Prayer – talk to God about all things.

2. New life in Christ – surrender your life to Jesus as Forgiver and Leader. You can do so by praying a simple prayer (which is just talking to God). For example: "Dear Lord Jesus, I know that I have sinned against you (sin is anything we think, say, or do that displeases God). Please forgive me for _____ (list your sins). Thank you for dying on the cross to pay for all my sins. I ask you to come into my life and be my Leader. Thank you for forgiving me, and giving me a place in heaven when I die. Amen

3. The Bible – read, memorize, and internalize God's love letter to you.

4. Good Books – can offer great counsel to you. (some suggestions are listed in Appendix 2)

5. Counsel – find a Christian counselor near you – call a local Bible-believing church, and ask for recommendations. "We are only as sick as our secrets."

6. Journaling – write your heart on paper. It's a way of sorting out feelings, writing prayers, and acknowledging hurt. It's a great way to say "hello" to your pain so you can also say "good-bye." It is also a great way to affirm who you are in Christ.

7. Church – find a Bible-believing church in your community. One that teaches that Jesus is the way to God and the Bible is the Word of God.

8. Small groups / a support group – a safe place with people who love you. It's an opportunity to journey along with others, who may be hurting as well. We were designed to live life together, not alone.

# Appendix 2

## A Bibliography on Sexual Abuse/ Addiction and Recovery

### Suggested Books:

| | |
|---|---|
| False Intimacy | Dr. Henry Schaumberg |
| Elizabeth's Legacy | Norma Smith |
| A Door of Hope | Jan Frank |
| A Silence to be Broken | Earl Wilson |
| Healing Victims of Sexual Abuse | Paula Sanford |
| Broken Image | Leanne Payne |
| Breaking Free | Russell Willingham |
| Helping Victims of Sexual Abuse | Lynn Heitritter, Jeanette Vought |

| | |
|---|---|
| Freeing Your Mind from Memories That Bind | Fred & Florence Littauer |
| Pain and Pretending | Rich Buhler |
| No Place to Cry: The Hurt and Healing of Sexual Abuse | Erwin Lutzer |
| Every Man's Battle | Steve Arterburn |
| Victory over the Darkness | Neil T. Anderson |

## Web Sites:

www.bethesdaworkshops.org

www.covenanteyes.com

www.pureintimacy.org

www.stonegateresouces.org

# Teresa Rilling

Teresa survived trauma and speaks passionately with humour about becoming all we were created to be. Her talks across Canada and beyond have been an inspiration to many.

She and Jim have been married since 1978 and reside in Alberta, Canada. They have three married children and eleven grandchildren. She loves to sing, play the piano and coffee with friends.

Printed in Canada